THE LITTLE BOOK OF big ideas ABOUT

ideas

ABOUT

Joy

elaine cannon

EAGLE
GATE

Eagle Gate is a registered trademark of Deseret Book Company.

Visit us at www.deseretbook.com

Library of Congress Catalog Card Number 00-133330

ISBN 1-57345-826-0

Printed in Mexico   18961-6721

10   9   8   7   6   5   4   3   2   1

J is for Joy! In ancient times this tenth letter of the alphabet was not recognized on its own. J descended from the vowel *iota* and the Semitic consonant *yod*, which was the first letter of the Hebrew word *Yahweh*. Because, in English, J became the first letter of the word *Jesus*, it was designed as the tallest capital letter in the type font. And Jesus is certainly *the* source of joy in our world today.

HAVE YOU FELT JOY?

There are some people who haven't. They haven't managed to differentiate between *lust* and *love*, let alone between *joy* and simply having *fun*. Others are just too busy to experience such a healing emotion. They don't see the brilliance of the setting sun, even when it's right in front of them. No wonder they've never been infused with joy! A few deprived souls may not even know that they are missing anything. Fools aplenty in today's world have been led astray by too little truth,

insufficient knowledge, false gods, feigned love, poor choices, and too much of nothing in particular.
But to miss the joy is to miss it all!

So let the joyful focus begin! The following pages will heighten your pleasure in people as well as sunsets—each one different—and in God and all his blessings that brim our cups. Just for the sheer joy of living fully, read on.

Elaine Cannon

THERE IS A FEELING, AN EXPERIENCE THAT IS

MORE DESIRABLE THAN ANY . . . CALL IT JOY.

IT IS MORE GRIPPING AND SATISFYING THAN

HAPPINESS. IT IS GRANDER THAN PLEASURE,

MORE LIFTING THAN FUN. IF YOU HAVE

HAD IT ONCE YOU WANT IT AGAIN.

Joy is a sometime thing, granted. There is hard work to be done, and there are battles to be won. But why settle for less when it is actually possible to achieve satisfaction in life, to delight in experiences, to wonder in discovery, to find tenderness in relationships? You *can* be surprised by joy when you've managed to stifle the skeptic within.

With only one

chance to live,

make it a good day

by expecting to

find joy in it.

Marcus Aurelius was a ruler with high ideals and a warring lifestyle who philosophized his way through disillusionment. Here is one of his great ideas: "Unhappy am I, because this has happened to me? Not so, but happy am I, though this has happened to me, because I continue free from pain, neither crushed by the present, nor fearing the future."

JOY IS MORE THAN PLEASURE, BETTER
THAN HAPPINESS, AND CANNOT BE
ENDURED AS A CONSTANT STATE. IT
IS RARE—A MOST BEAUTIFUL, EXUL-
TANT EMOTION. IT IS TO BE HANDLED
WITH FULL FOCUS, AND TREASURED.

I ECHO THE WISDOM OF PRESIDENT

GORDON B. HINCKLEY, WHO HINTS

THAT JOY IS THE FLIP SIDE OF CYNICISM

WHEN HE SAYS: "I AM ASKING THAT WE

STOP SEEKING OUT THE STORMS AND

ENJOY MORE FULLY THE SUNLIGHT . . .

THAT AS WE GO THROUGH LIFE, WE

'ACCENTUATE THE POSITIVE,' . . . LOOK A

LITTLE DEEPER FOR THE GOOD, THAT WE

STILL OUR VOICES OF INSULT AND SARCASM,

THAT WE MORE GENEROUSLY COMPLIMENT

AND ENDORSE VIRTUE AND EFFORT."

My own joy surfaced in a mature sense

when I was young and the ideal of serving

the Lord by helping others was fresh upon me.

I had my motto lifted from the printed page

to the artistry of calligraphy, framed under

glass to guard my desk, where it is still:

"Perhaps I may be an instrument in

the hands of God to bring some soul to

repentance; and this is my joy."

(ALMA 29:9)

Sweet new Millennium

Before thee lies,

The world is born again.

Endless possibilities

Beneath innocent skies—accept life—

Forward then.

Come, Joy!

JOY IS SYNONYMOUS WITH GOD'S BEAUTIFUL

CREATIONS: A DEER FEEDING IN WINTER

BEYOND THE KITCHEN WINDOW, FIRST

VIOLETS BRAVING A FROST, A RADIANT

NEWBORN OF THE ROYAL GENERATION

SAVED TO COME FORTH NOW.

Ah! Joy is Paul Engle's wonder of love:

"Seeing you there

is like

finding a snowflake

on the palm of my hand in July."

I am in harmony with William
Wordsworth, who wrote:
My heart leaps up when I behold
A rainbow in the sky:
So was it when my life began;
So is it now I am a man;
So be it when I shall grow old,
Or let me die!

Have you personally noticed that true love and joy come from the same warm heart full of understanding that God *is* love, gives love, and sweetens our love?

GOD IS AWARE AND MINDFUL OF ORDINARY

PEOPLE, HIS CHILDREN ALL.

God keeps his promises, he helps us keep

ours with him, and thus know joy.

A SMALL GIRL DRESSED UP IN HER

HALLOWEEN COSTUME—A SALVATION

ARMY SANTA CLAUS, COMPLETE WITH

THE RELENTLESS TINGLE-TINGLE OF A

BELL ON A LONG BLACK , HANDLE—

AND WENT ON HER WAY FOR TREATS.

HER BAG WAS FULL WHEN SHE

KNOCKED ON THE LAST DOOR.

THE LADY OF THE HOUSE EXPRESSED SORROW THAT HER STORE OF GOODIES WAS EMPTY. EVERY LAST COOKIE HAD BEEN HANDED OUT.

"THAT'S OKAY," SAID THE YOUNG SANTA MERRILY, " I HAVE PLENTY IN MY SACK, AND I'LL GIVE YOU SOME OF MINE."

Think of the poignant prospect of finding

out from what roots one has come—

English Lords and Ladies; first Christian

missionaries in New Zealand; rope twister

from New England; Pony Express rider;

fiddler for dancing round the circle of

pioneer wagons; a maker of silk bonnets;

a writer of sonnets; an engraver from Oslo.

Whatever your earliest beginnings, when

you recognize them, plant them in the core

of you, where joy springs.

It is no small thing to have bonded in a family where people are friends as well as relatives; where that company is preferred; where those memories made are favorite ones; where traditions fortify passing years; and where the connecting lines *fore and aft,* as Benjamin Franklin described genealogy, are valued in the marvelous joy of belonging.

At our son's funeral we found comfort—
and a nudge—in Elder Neal A. Maxwell's
remarks: "The adversity that we see borne
so well [in this life] has to do with our
capacity for joy in the next world."

Wasn't it some ancient god who
questioned the newcomer in his heaven, "Did
you find joy? Did you bring joy?"

Will you?

Trust joy.

Allow it to happen.

Put yourself in situations of such a nature that psychological readiness permits *recognition* of the sacred nature of the feeling until your spiritual side *receives* joy!

Joy can be the bonus to a deliberate attitude of peace, which a tenth century Hindu prayer suggests:

"Peaceful be earth, peaceful heaven, peaceful waters, peaceful trees. I render peaceful whatever here is terrible, whatever here is cruel, whatever here is sinful. Let it become auspicious; let everything be beneficial to us."

Go for joy in life as pointedly as

a produce farmer would reach

for the best peach on the tree.

Meeting Helen Keller in person, for me, was an avenue to joy. Blind and deaf since birth, she uttered these famous words about how to find joy: "I who am blind can give one hint to those who see. Use your eyes as if tomorrow you would be stricken blind. And the same method can be applied to the other senses. Hear the music of voices, the song of a bird, the mighty strains of an orchestra as if you would be stricken deaf tomorrow. Touch each object as if tomorrow your tactile sense would fail. Smell the perfume of flowers, taste with relish each morsel as if tomorrow you could never smell and taste again."

She spoke of what she would focus on if she could have but one day to see. Hearing that, I wondered, *what if that one day it rained?* She would rejoice in rain. Of course!

THE FOURTH VERSE OF THE THIRD
EPISTLE OF JOHN IS A FAVORITE WITH
CONSCIENTIOUS, GODFEARING PARENTS,
"I HAVE NO GREATER JOY THAN TO
HEAR THAT MY CHILDREN WALK IN
TRUTH." HOWEVER, GIVEN THEIR BUSY
LIFESTYLE AND FAR, SCATTERED PLACES,
IT WOULD BE MY JOY EVEN TO SEE THEM.

Oh the joy—the inexpressible joy—
of feeling safe with someone who will
take you as you are, blowing away the
chaff, appreciating the grain!

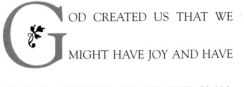

GOD CREATED US THAT WE MIGHT HAVE JOY AND HAVE IT FULL FOREVER. THAT'S THE PLAN.

OUR PART IS TO BELIEVE THE PLANNER.

Joy is a bonus of witnessing true beauty. My recollection of real beauty was the fall after I had been baptized. Walking up the hill home from the neighborhood store we had a perfect view of a splendid crisp spring sunset over Great Salt Lake. Coral clouds flung across the sky like a grand striped fan. I went home and drew it from memory to the best of my eight-year-old ability and labeled it *Joy!*

IT IS A WELCOME FLOOD OF JOY TO

THINK OF CHILDHOOD AND HAVE IT

COME FORTH CLEARLY—SO CLEARLY

AS TO FEEL MY FATHER'S WARMTH AS

HE CARRIED ME HALF-ASLEEP FROM

THE CAR TO MY BED AFTER LAGOON.

Comfort that surpasses all understanding of possibility responds quickly to a prayer of invitation. With it comes indescribable joy in Christ—that same Christ who was born of Mary by God. He lived. He taught. He showed the way. Crucified, he died but he rose. He lives again. Having this kind of faith brings joy.

A beloved gentleman of great civic
contribution once said, "I'd give
anything if I had a testimony."
"Ask," the Master Teacher coaxed.
Then, joy!

JOY COMES FROM SWEET REUNIONS,

MEMORIES REVISITED, AND FAVORITE

SCRIPTURES RE-READ.

There was a sacred meeting of

loved ones after the naming

and father's blessing of a firstborn

beauty straight from heaven.

Gladness was so full among par-

ents, siblings, grandparents, and

"grandmother great" that voices

were raised in a hymn of praise:

"Oh, how joyful it will be when our Savior we shall see! When in splendor he'll descend, then all wickedness will end . . . every living thing therein shall in love and beauty dwell; then with joy each heart will swell."

(*HYMNS*, NO. 58.)

To reap joy out of the inevitable, believe that the Creator of us all knows the workings of our souls and our mortal machines. Every one is part of the Master's plan. Each participates in the basics— birthing, growing, knowing self, mating, enduring, and loving anyway. Then, at last each is crowned by joy, loving in gratitude rather than expectation of constancy amid change.

"I have overcome the world,"

Jesus said. Ultimate joy also rests

upon our own such achievement.

We live in a day of wonder and joy as temples

dot the earth, as good people hear prophets in

prayers of dedication to God regarding holy work

in sacred buildings. At the dedication of the

house of David a song was sung by King David

that could, perhaps, be repeated by some today:
"I will extol thee, O Lord; for thou hast lifted me
up, and hast not made my foes to rejoice over me.
O Lord my God, I cried unto thee, and thou hast
healed me. . . . brought up my soul from the grave.
. . . Sing unto the Lord, O ye saints of his, and
give thanks at the remembrance of his holiness.
For his anger endureth but a moment; in his
favour is life: weeping may endure for a night,
but joy cometh in the morning" (PSALM 30:1–5).

Read and rejoice in the story of

Samuel, the child Hannah prayed to

bear. When her prayers were answered

she praised God in joy and took the child

to the temple and lent him to the Lord.

The story continues:

"The Lord called Samuel: and he answered,
Here am I. . . . And the Lord called yet again,
Samuel. . . . Then Samuel answered, Speak;
for thy servant heareth" (1 SAMUEL 3:4–10).

Insert your own name in place of Samuel's
to remember how you felt when you were
called—surely called—to serve the Lord.
And *you* knew joy!

There follows a powerful formula

for feeling joy even when it's dark

during sun-is-up time:

"Believe in God; believe that he is,

and that he created all things, both

in heaven and in earth; believe that

he has all wisdom, and all power,

both in heaven and in earth; believe

that man doth not comprehend all

the things which the Lord can

comprehend" (MOSIAH 4:9).

If you have come to know God, and
have received forgiveness from sin,
such remission will bring exceedingly
great joy in your soul until you retain
a remembrance of the greatness of
God and his inevitable, inimitable
love for you—not because you are
great, but because he is.

HERE ARE SOME HAND-IN-HAND,

GO-WITH WORDS FOR JOY:

ENJOYED, JOYFUL, JOYOUS, LIGHT,

HAPPINESS, GLADNESS, WELL-

BEING, LOVE RECIPROCATED.

At Christmastime, a couple from North

Carolina sent a greeting card (a literal

card sans envelope so all the world could

read and rejoice) with words in green:

As again we kneel

Before the cradled Christ

Let hope be rekindled,

Let love for all abound,

Let there be joy!

OFTEN JOY IS A PERSONAL EXPERIENCE; THOUGH

PEOPLE MAY FEEL IT TOGETHER WHEN A TENDER,

GOD-BLESSED MOMENT IS AT HAND. EACH MAY

RESPOND IN A DIFFERENT WAY, OR ALL MAY BE

MOVED, WITHOUT COMMAND, TO WEEP, CLAP,

SHOUT, PRAY, SING, BE SPEECHLESS, OR PRAISE

GOD FROM WHOM ALL THE BEST BLESSINGS FLOW.

A favorite phrase with which to comfort and inspire: "Well done, good and faithful servant . . . enter thou into the joy of thy lord" (MATTHEW 25:23).

I remember a spring drenched with rain, promising a stunning green for a season in the Rockies, the foothills, the fields, and parks. Then the fruit trees prettied up the scene everywhere. In joy, I thought of the gift of fruit in late summer and fall and prayed against a killing frost. There is a simile in Galatians 5:22: "But the fruit of the Spirit is love, joy, peace, longsuffering, gentleness, goodness, faith." Fruit for the body, yes, but what a wonderful blessing is God's fruit for the soul!

WILLIAM WORDSWORTH WAS MY
FAVORITE POET FOR ONE WHOLE
QUARTER OF COLLEGE ENGLISH. I
RECOGNIZED IN HIM MY OWN LOVE OF
NATURE—THE HOST OF DAFFODILS,
THE RAINBOW, THE PLACE OF JOY
NEXT TO GOD. HE WAS "SURPRISED
BY JOY—IMPATIENT AS THE WIND."

I am *not* surprised by joy, I expect it—because of my training in Christ and my life experiences with his great giving and forgiving heart.

And if the rising and setting of the sun right on schedule every day doesn't stir in your heart faith and joy, get away to some open space at night and gaze into the incredible wonder of a sea of sparkling stars—the ongoing birthplace of constellations.

"Joy to the world,

the Lord is come;

Let earth receive her King!"

Sooner rather than later.

THANKS TO THE DEAR LORD

THAT WE CAN LEARN FROM

SHARED EXPERIENCES. JOY

COMES WHEN STANDING UPON

THE SHOULDERS OF OTHERS.

about the author

❧

Elaine Cannon continues to bring impressive experience, insight, and delight in her writing. In her long career, Mrs. Cannon has authored more than fifty books and has received numerous honors and awards for her work.

ISBN 1-57345-826-0